AngularJS Mastery

A Code-Like-a-Pro Guide for AngularJS Beginners

CONTENTS

INTRODUCTION

I want to thank you and congratulate you for downloading the book, "AngularJS Mastery: A Code-Like-a-Pro Guide for AngularJS Beginners". This book contains proven steps and strategies on how to build powerful and dynamic web applications using this popular JavaScript framework. Learn the theory and principals behind AngularJS as you follow along with this easy step-by-step guide to web application development.

Thanks again for downloading this book, I hope you enjoy it!

CHAPTER 1: WHAT EXACTLY IS ANGULARJS?

In the constellation of JavaScript frameworks that are now available, AngularJS provides a package of functions that allow to developers to design fast and powerful web applications capable of handling large data files. AngularJS is an open source web application framework. AngularJS helps web developers create programming logic for their applications within the actual web page, and link the web application data model to backend databases and services. This exciting program scripting language also allows UI design logic to be expressed in an HTML template file. This is particularly useful for the presentation of data. AngularJS provides helpful structure for web development and streamlines the entire process of designing and testing web-based applications. By learning AngularJS, you will be able to create interactive web applications with well-structured code that is simple to update and maintain.

AngularJS is a JavaScript framework for creating dynamic web apps. It expands the capabilities of an HTML template, enabling designers to turn static web pages into fully interactive web applications. AngularJS uses the concepts of data binding and dependency injection in ways that greatly reduce the amount of code that would be required with other web programming languages.

- It accomplishes this through the generation new HTML structures. Angular helps the web browser to interpret original syntax by using various directives, including:
- Data binding
- Object control structures for replicating elements of the web page.
- Generating and validating user forms.
- Giving DOM elements new behaviors.
- Organizing and reusing HTML components.

By using the AngularJS JavaScript framework, you will be able to create powerful, easy to maintain web applications. Web developers use the Model View Controller (MVC) model when coding in AngularJS. This programing language is popular among web developers partly because AngularJS works with JavaScript in any browser, and the AngularJS library is open source and completely free.

A Code-Like-a-Pro Guide for AngularJS Beginners

CHAPTER 2: ADVANTAGES OF ANGULARJS

Some advantages of AngularJS include:

- The ability to make well-organized single-page applications.
- The ability to bind data to HTML.
- Testable code.
- Separation of component responsibilities.
- Reusable components.
- Greater functionality with shorter code.
- Compatibility with all major browsers and mobile devices.

Disadvantages of AngularJS

- AngularJS is not secure: Because the entire framework consists of JavaScript, the data stored in AngularJS applications are not secure.
- AngularJS is not degradable: If JavaScript is disabled in the user's browser, the application will not work.

CHAPTER 3: SETTING UP YOUR DEVELOPMENT ENVIRONMENT

We need the following tools to setup a development environment for AngularJS:

In order to work along with this book, you will need to set up your AngularJS development environment. For this you will need:

- Text Editor/IDE
- Browser
- Web server
- AngularJS Library

Text Editor/IDE
AngularJS is ultimately comprised of HTML and JavaScript, therefore any standard text editor/IDE will do. You might consider one of the following free programs:
- Notepad++
- Sublime Text
- Aptana Studio 3
- Ultra Edit
- Text Wrangler
- Eclipse
- Visual Studio

*You can also use online editors, such as jsbin.com or plnkr.com.

Web server
If you will be developing on your local computer, you may use such web servers as Apache or MS IIS.

Web Browser
Any major browser such as Chrome, Firefox, or Safari will work for this purpose, and AngularJS cross-browser compatible. Just make sure that JavaScript is enabled.

AngularJS Library

Downloading AngularJS

Click on link: **https://angularjs.org/**.

There are three options to download AngularJS library:

- **View on GitHub**- By clicking on this button, you can download and install the library for direct use from your server.
- **Download Version 1**
- **Download Version 2**

If you would like to download a library, select Version 1.

Using the Content Delivery Network

Because AngularJS is JavaScript library, the only thing necessary to work with AngularJS in your environment is to provide the application access to the angular.js library file with a <script> tag in the HTML templates. This can be done by using the Content Delivery Network (CDN), which supplies a URL for downloading the library from an online source, such Google's (<script src="https://ajax.googleapis.com/ajax/libs/angularjs/1.2.5/angular.min.js"> </script>). If the application cannot connect to the source, it will not work. Another way to supply the angular.js library is to directly download it from (**http://angularjs.org**) and provide the library through your web server. This slows down the application, but is more reliable. We will use the online CDN library throughout this book.

Bootstrapping AngularJS

In order to use AngularJS in your web application you must include the following Script. <**script src="http://code.angularjs.org/1.0.5/angular.js"> </script>**. The browser both loads and executes this file at the same time. Each segment of AngularJS code in your application works as a singlular function, and the last line included in the script enacts that particular function. (function(window, document, undefined) {'use strict';......// All of your application's AngularJS code is written here.})(window, document); //the last line in your code tells the browser to begin the function.

Every AngularJS function requires an object for the particular HTML location that the code is written in. When the object is identified, the AngularJS "DOMContentLoaded" event listener sends a callback to initiate execution of all the function's directives. Once AngularJS receives a callback, indicating the the object has been loaded, it looks to the "ng-app directive" to learn which HTML elements will be affected by the function. The instructions are then executed for that specific function, and it begins enacting the directives. AngularJS refers to this whole process as "Automatic Initialization."

There are two parts to this process. The first part involves using the ng-app directive to define the application module. This directive (typically loaded in the <html> tag) signals the compiler to consider it the root. The second part is to load the angular.js library with the aforementioned <script> tag. The ng-app directive is to ensure that the entire web page is included; however, you could add it to another container element, and only elements inside that container would be included in the AngularJS compilation and consequently in the AngularJS application functionality.

AngularJS includes an HTML complier that looks for directives in the AngularJS template and uses JavaScript directive code to create extended HTML elements. The HTML compiler enables you to teach the browser new HTML syntax. It also allows you to assign behaviors to any HTML elements or attributes. In fact, you can even design new HTML elements or attributes that have unique behaviors. These HTML extensions are called directives. Angular has many built-in directives that are helpful with building any app. All of the directives are executed by the web browser, eliminating any need for no server side coding.

- Compile: Search the HTML object and collect all of the instructions (directives).
- Link: Combine the directives with a scope (data) and produce a live view for the user. All changes to the scope model are projected in the view. All user interactions changes to the view are updated in the scope model as well.

The compiler loads into the web browser when the library is bootstrapped. Once it is loaded, the compiler will look through the HTML, tie in any back-end JavaScript code to the web page elements, and render the client view for the application user. Because the compiler searches for directives as soon as the angular.js script is loaded, it is best practice to include the angular.js library as one of the last tags in the <body> of the HTML, which helps the web page to load more quickly.

Example (Loading the Library)

```
<!doctype html>
<html ng-app="myApp">
 <body>
 <script src="http://code.angularjs.org/1.2.9/angular.min.js"></script>
  <script src="/lib/myApp.js"></script>
  </body>
</html>
```

CHAPTER 4: THE SPA CONCEPT

Unlike traditional desktop computer applications, web applications are designed to operate on a variety of operating systems and devices. They have the advantage of being easily deployed and implemented anywhere with an Internet connection. Most web applications are built using frameworks that are composed of JavaScript.

A Single Page Application (SPA) is a full application that functions entirely within a web browser. Because they consist of single web pages, SPA do not require pages to reload during a client session.

SPA Features

Web pages in SPAs are generated dynamically. That allows for custom presentations and experiences based upon user interaction with the application. SPAs are not restricted to linear pathways from URL to URL throughout a website. They function on the MVC model (explained later in the book) which allows a controller to determine the sequence of page presentations, based on user interactions.

All user interactions result in the creation and loading of various sections of the web page.

This is all regulated by built-in AngularJS components that are specially designed to perform separate parts of the process.

The dynamically-generated web pages can be loaded at different times with content from different servers, because AngularJS uses AJAX (Asynchronous JavaScript and XML), a web programming protocol.

AngularJS stands above web apps that rely on the server-templating model, by using its application web server to handle changing data and incorporating it into the HTML. When a interacts with the webpage, either an HTTP POST or an HTTP GET operation is performed on the web server, resulting in a new HTML being passed to the browser and rendered for the user.

A Code-Like-a-Pro Guide for AngularJS Beginners

CHAPTER 5: THE MVC MODEL

- Model to represent current state of your application
- View to display the data
- Controller that controls the relation between Models and Views.

The AngularJS framework is based on the MVC (Model View Controller) model. With this framework, developers can make powerful applications that are highly structured, relatively easy to understand, and simple to maintain. The MVC model has three components: the Model (which is the data source), the View (which is what is seen on the webpage), and the Controller (which regulates interactions between the Model and the View). The MVC model is designed to separate Java Script (JS) tasks, which helps to keep your JS code organized and understandable.
We will take a closer look at each component.

MVC Architecture

A benefit of MVC is that it separates the application logic from the user interface and compartmentalizes concerns. The controller obtains application requests and helps the model prepare data needed for the view. Thus it separates the business logic, presentation logic and navigation logic. The view, in turn, uses the data delivered by the controller to render a client presentation. Below is a graphic representation of this model.

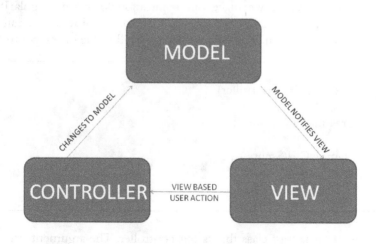

The model
The model manages the application data by responding to requests from view and controller to update itself.

The view
This is a rendered presentation of data for the client/user. The view is activated by the controller's instructions to present data. Many script-based systems such as JSP, ASP, PHP and relatively simple to integrate with AJAX (Asynchronous JavaScript and XML) technology.
The controller
The controller operates in response to user input. It receives user requests, builds the model object, and passes that object to the view.

Model
A model in AngularJS can be a string, number, boolean or any JavaScript object. The model exists inside of the controller.

View
The view is what the client sees within an HTML element. With AngularJS the view is an object in the Document Object Model (DOM) that displays data from the controller. AngularJS uses two-way data binding (discussed later in this book), wherein the view updates automatically when there are model changes in the model. You do not have to write special code to handle this process; the controller takes care of it automatically.

Controller
The controller is where we place our application logic. In AngularJS, a controller is formed by javascript classes. Controllers allow us to call for components to work with. The data model is placed inside of the controller.

Example (Creating the Controller)

Listing 1: Creating first controller

```
function ExampleCtrl($scope) {
    // controller code here
}
```

This creates a JavaScript class that is our controller. The argument with the dollar sign ($) is called a scope, and one is needed for every controller that we create. The purpose of the scope is to bind together the controller and view.

Model Creation
The model is also a regular JavaScript object that lives inside of the controller. The model is available to the view, because it is bound be the control's scope ($scope) as explained earlier.

Example

Creation of models.

```
function ExampleCtrl($scope) {
     // model called 'welcome' which is a string
     $scope.welcome = "Hello, AngularJS Students!";
     var users = [
{name: "Micky", point: 45 },
{name: "Tim", point: 85},
{name: "Susy", point: 55}
];

     // model called 'students' which is an array of objects
     $scope.students = students;
}
```

In the above code, we create our first model called 'welcome' which is a string and a model called 'students', which is an object array. Because we want the model data to be synchronized with our view, we make each model as a property of $scope.

Completing the View
Now that we have set up our controller and defined the models, we must create a view to display the data to the user. Because view is the Document Object Model (DOM), we write the view just as if we were writing normal HTML, and we will add an expression.

Example (Creating a View)

```
<!DOCTYPE html>
```

```html
<html ng-app>
<head>
 <title>Welcome to AngularJS</title>
</head>
<body>
    <div ng-controller="ExampleCtrl">
        <h1>{{welcome}}</h1>
        <ol>
            <li ng-repeat="students in students">{{student.name}} -
{{student.point}}</li>
</ol>
    </div>
<script
src="https://ajax.googleapis.com/ajax/libs/angularjs/1.0.7/angular.min.js
"></script>
<script>
function ExampleCtrl($scope) {
    // model called 'welcome' which is a string
    $scope.welcome = "Hello, Angular is awesome!";

    var users = [
{name: "Micky", point: 45 },
{name: "Tim", point: 85},
{name: "Suzy", point: 55}
];

    // model called 'student' which is an array of objects
    $scope.users = students;
}
</script>
</body>
</html>
```

We now have our MVC model with our data, client presentation, and mechanism for keeping both automatically synced. This is the first step to completing a functional AngularJS application. Next, we will learn the basic components, their purposes, their specific responsibilities, and the ways in which they interact together. We will now examine the conceptual components of an AngularJS application.

A Code-Like-a-Pro Guide for AngularJS Beginners

CHAPTER 6: ANGULARJS CONCEPTS

The following diagram depicts key AngularJS elements that will be discussed in this book.

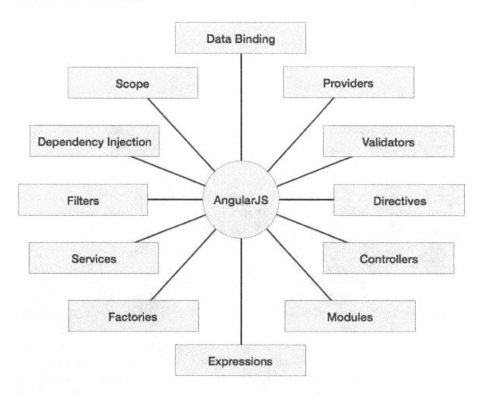

Core Features

Core features of AngularJS include:

- **Expressions**: JavaScript instructions telling the app what to do.
- **Data-binding**: The automatic synchronization of data between model (backend) and view (frontend) components.
- **Scope**: Objects that maintain continuity between the controller and view.
- **Controller**: JS functions linked to a specific scope.
- **Services**: Objects that are instantiated only one time per session.
- **Filters**: Function to select subsets of items from arrays.
- **Directives**: Markers on Document Object Model (DOM) elements that can be used to generate custom HTML tags.
- **Templates**: Fully-rendered views containing information from the

controller and model.
- **Routing**: The method used for switching views.
- **Model View Controller (MVC)**: This is a pattern of dividing an application into the following components: the Model, the View, and the Controller. These components all have specific responsibilities.
- **Deep Linking**: Deep linking encodes the state of an application in the URL, so that it may be restored to the same state from the URL in a new session.
- **Dependency Injection**: A built-in subsystem to help with the development and testing of AngularJS applications.

Views

In AngularJS, every HTML element is represented by a DOM (Document Object Model) object. The browser reads DOM object properties and renders the HTML element on the page.
Dynamic web applications typically utilize JavaScript or a JavaScript-based libraries, such as jQuery to present DOM objects in their rendered behavior and appearance based on DOM properties. The final rendered product is called the view. The number of possible views in a single web page are unlimited.

Expressions

AngularJS includes the ability to place data expressions inside of HTML elements. AngularJS evaluates expressions and dynamically projects the result to a client view. Since expressions are tied to the scope, expression can utilizes values in the scope. As the data model changes, so do the values of the expression. Expressions can be enclosed inside double braces: {{ *expression* }}. They can also be written inside of a directive: ng-bind="expression". Once expressions are executed, the controller sends the results to the HTML location where the expression is written. Like JavaScript expressions, these can include literals, operators, and variables.

Example (Expressions)

```
<!DOCTYPE html>
<html>
<script
src="http://ajax.googleapis.com/ajax/libs/angularjs/1.4.8/angular.min.js"
></script>
<body>
<div ng-app>
<p>Example Expression: {{10 - 8 }}</p>
```

18

A Code-Like-a-Pro Guide for AngularJS Beginners

```
</div>
</body>
</html>
```

Output

Example Expression: 2

Angular Expressions vs. JavaScript Expressions
- Angular expressions are like JavaScript expressions with the following differences:
- Context: JavaScript expressions are interpreted globally throughout the application. AngularJS expressions are evaluated within the scope of an object.
- Trying to evaluate undefined properties In JavaScript results in "ReferenceError" or "TypeError." AngularJS expression evaluation simply results in "undefined" and "null."
- No Control Flow Statements: AngularJS does not have these common programming expressions: "conditionals", "loops", or "exceptions".
- No Function Declarations: Functions cannot be declared in AngularJS expressions, not even within the ng-init directive.

For more complex JavaScript code, you can create a controller method that is initiated from the client view.

Modules

Everything in your AngularJS app is contained inside of a module. They are used to hold onto controllers and other relevant code about our application. Placing code inside of different modules protects the code from being considered "global" in scope, giving you more control over your app's functioning. A module represents components in an application. It is a type of container for the for the application controllers. The name given to a module helps you to reference scopes, directives, and other components of the application. Named modules a very useful for the packaging and reuse of an applications various elements. The ng-app directive assigns every web page and view or to a specific module.

Example_(Modules)

```
<div ng-app="exampleApp">...</div>
<script>
var app = angular.module("myApp", []);
</script>
```

Adding a Controller

Now we will add a controller to our application, by referring to the controller with the ng-controllerdirective:

Example (Controller Directive)

```
<!DOCTYPE html>
<html>
<script
src="http://ajax.googleapis.com/ajax/libs/angularjs/1.4.8/angular.min.js"
></script>
<body>
<div ng-app="exampleApp" ng-controller="exampleCtrl">
{{ first+ " " + last }}
</div>
<script>
var app = angular.module("exampleApp", []);
app.controller("exampleCtrl", function($scope) {
    $scope.firstName = "eBook";
    $scope.last_name = "Reader";
});
</script>
</body>
</html>
```

Output
eBook Reader

Directives
   Directives help to bring AngularJS applications to life. Directives are used to create original syntax, and each begins with the prefix ng- (which stands for "Angular"). A directive is assigned to give a DOM element a special behavior. For example, "ng-repeat" repeats a specific element and "ng-show" shows an element only under certain conditions. The idea behind

directives is simply that it makes your HTML truly interactive by attaching event listeners (objects that initiate actions in response to other actions) to the elements and taking action on the assigned DOM. AngularJS includes a variety of useful built-in directives, but it is also useful to create custom directives for your individual needs. You can also create your own directives. The ng-app directive begins an AngularJS application. The ng-init directive starts the application data. The ng-model directive syncs the value of the user input controls to application data. You can create custom directives, however it is best practice not to use the "ng" prefix, due to possible conflicts.

Example (Directives)

```
<!DOCTYPE html>
<html>
<script
src="http://ajax.googleapis.com/ajax/libs/angularjs/1.4.8/angular.min.js"
></script>
<body>
<div ng-app="exampleApp" Example-directive></div>
<script>
var app = angular.module("exampleApp", []);
app.directive("exampleDirective", function() {
    return {
        template : "example directive constructor"
    };
});
</script>
</body>
</html>
```

Output

Example directive constructor

The ng-model Directive
This directive syncs the value of HTML controls to the data. The directive "ng-model" enables you to tie an input value to a variable created in your app.

Example (Directives)

```
<!DOCTYPE html>
<html>
<script
src="http://ajax.googleapis.com/ajax/libs/angularjs/1.4.8/angular.min.js"
></script>
<body>
<div ng-app="myApp" ng-controller="exampleCtrl">
Name: <input ng-model="name">
</div>
<script>
var app = angular.module('exampleApp', []);
app.controller('exampleCtrl', function($scope) {
    $scope.name = "eBook Reader";
});
</script>
<p>This is the ng-model directive.</p>
</body>
</html>
```

Output

Name: [   ]
This is the ng-model directive

AngularJS allows you to combine templates with different directives, so that you can combine the HTML with the JavaScript for dynamic and unique displays. This greatly extends the capabilities of HTML. Directives are divided into two parts. Part 1 includes: CSS classes, added attributes, and elements that are added to HTML. The second part includes JavaScript, which extends the behavior of the HTML.

A popular feature of AngularJS is the built-in AngularJS directives that handle most of the DOM manipulation needed to sync the contents of the scope with elements in the client view.

You can design your own custom directives to add functionality to you web application.

Data Binding

Integrated data binding is perhaps the most popular feature of AngularJS. Data binding is the synchronization between the view and the data model. The data binding process ties together data from the model (the collection of data available for the application) together with the view (elements in the web page). With AngularJS, data is bound in both directions. As data is entered through the web page, the backend data model is updated, and when data is modified in the back end model, the web page is automatically updated. In this way, current data in the model is always accurately represented to the user, making the view a simple projection of the model.

Example (Data Binding)

```
var app = angular.module('exampleApp', []);
app.controller('exampleCtrl', function($scope) {
    $scope.firstname = "eBook";
    $scope.last_name = "Reader";
});
```

HTML View
The web page container where the application objects and data are displayed for the user, is called the view. The view is linked to the model through the process of data binding. One way to displaying model data in the view is to use the ng-bind directive.

Example (HTML View)

```
<!DOCTYPE html>
<html>
<script
src="http://ajax.googleapis.com/ajax/libs/angularjs/1.4.8/angular.min.js"
></script>
<body>
<div ng-app="exampleApp" ng-controller="exampleCtrl">
    <p ng-bind="lasttname"></p>
</div>
<script>
var app = angular.module('exampleApp', []);
app.controller('exampleCtrl', function($scope) {
    $scope.firstname = "eBook";
    $scope.last_name = "Reader";
});
```

```
</script>
```
<p>The ng-bind directive to sync the HTML elements to the data model.</p>
```
</body>
</html>
```

Output
The ng-bind directive to sync the HTML elements to the data model.

You can also use double braces {{ }} to display content from the model (e.g. name: {{last_name}}).

Two-way Binding

Data binding in AngularJS involves bringing together the model (data) and the view (what the user sees). When data in the model changes, the view reflects the change, and when data in the view changes, the model is updated as well. This happens simultaneously, keeping the model and the view in sync at all times. Two-way data binding is a way to accomplish this synchronization. Any change happens in the back-end happens in the front-end and vice versa. This process allows you to achieve high performance in your web application with significantly less effort than it would take in any other programming or coding language. To accomplish this in jQuery, you would have to code logic in both the model and view. However, in AngularJS the $scope does the work for you.

Example (Two-Way Binding)

```
<!DOCTYPE html>
<html>
<script
src="http://ajax.googleapis.com/ajax/libs/angularjs/1.4.8/angular.min.js"
></script>
<body>
<div ng-app="exampleApp" ng-controller="exampleCtrl">
   Name: <input ng-model="laststname">
   <h1>{{last_name}}</h1>
</div>
<script>
var app = angular.module('exampleApp', []);
app.controller('exampleCtrl', function($scope) {
   $scope.firstname = "eBook";
```

```
    $scope.last_name = "Reader";
});
</script>
<p>When you change the name inside of the input field, the model data
will change automatically, and so will the header.</p>
</body>
</html>
```

Output
Name:

Reader

When you change the name inside of the input field, the model data will change automatically, and so will the header.

Controllers

A Controller is an object that manages other objects in the app. The controller does not know specifics about the object it controls, however it knows how to access the object, how to get information about it, or how to pass it to the view for display. If your application has an object such as a student, it will also have a studentController. The MVC framework is completed through *controllers*. These controllers are used to regulate the data and flow of AngularJS applications. Controllers are added to HTML elements through directives that are implement as JavaScript Objects, which contain properties and functions. They supplement the application's scope by establishing its state and by giving it specific behaviors. The ng-controller directive is used to define the AngularJS controller. The $scope parameter, refers to the application or module which is to be handled by a specific controller. Because the model and the view are synchronized, a controller can be totally separated from the view and simply operate on the model data. Due to AngularJS data binding in, the view will always reflect changes made in the controller.

Example (Controller)

```
<!DOCTYPE html>
<html>
<script
src="http://ajax.googleapis.com/ajax/libs/angularjs/1.4.8/angular.min.js"
></script>
```

```
<body>
<div ng-app="exampleApp" ng-controller="exampleCtrl">
First Name: <input type="text" ng-model="firstName"><br>
Last_Name: <input type="text" ng-model="last_name"><br>
<br>
Full Name: {{firstName + " " + last_name}}
</div>
<script>
var app = angular.module('exampleApp', []);
app.controller('exampleCtrl', function($scope) {
    $scope.firstName = "eBook";
    $scope.last_name = "Reader";
});
</script>
</body>
</html>
```

Output

First Name:

Last_Name:

Full Name: eBook Reader

The AngularJS application is defined by ng-app="myApp". The application runs inside the <div>. The ng-controller="exampleCtrl" attribute is an AngularJS directive. It defines a controller.

The exampleCtrl function is a JavaScript function. AngularJS will invoke the controller with a $scope object. In AngularJS, $scope is the application object (the owner of application variables and functions). The controller creates two properties (variables) in the scope (firstName and last_name). The ng-model directives bind the input fields to the controller properties (firstName and last_name).

Controller Methods

The example above demonstrated a controller object with two properties: last_name and firstName. A controller can also have methods (variables as functions):

Example (Controller Method)

A Code-Like-a-Pro Guide for AngularJS Beginners

```html
<!DOCTYPE html>
<html>
<script
src="http://ajax.googleapis.com/ajax/libs/angularjs/1.4.8/angular.min.js"
></script>
<body>
<div ng-app="exampleApp" ng-controller="exampleCtrl">
First: <input type="text" ng-model="firstName"><br>
Last: <input type="text" ng-model="last_name"><br>
<br>
Full Name: {{fullName()}}
</div>
<script>
var app = angular.module('exampleApp', []);
app.controller('exampleCtrl', function($scope) {
   $scope.firstName = "eBook";
   $scope.last_name = "Reader";
   $scope.fullName = function() {
      return $scope.firstName + " " + $scope.last_name;
   };
});
</script>
</body>
</html>
```

Output

First:

Last:

Full Name: eBook Reader

Scopes

The scope syncs the HTML (view) and the JavaScript (controller). This is an object with the accessible properties and methods. It is accessible to both the view and the controller, which passes the object in the $scope as an argument. As your application first begins, AngularJS generates the "$rootScope." As the scope searches the DOM, it finds and processes directives, some of which (such as "ng-controller") request new scopes.

Once compilation is complete, AngularJS will have produced a scope tree replica of the DOM tree. Separate scopes allow for different parts of the view to separate their presentations of the data model.

Example (Scope)

```
<!DOCTYPE html>
<html>
<script
src="http://ajax.googleapis.com/ajax/libs/angularjs/1.4.8/angular.min.js"
></script>
<body>
<div ng-app="exampleApp" ng-controller="exampleCtrl">
<h1>{{state}}</h1>
</div>
<script>
var app = angular.module('exampleApp', []);
app.controller('exampleCtrl', function($scope) {
   $scope.state = "California";
});
</script>
</body>
</html>
```

Output

California

When you add properties to the $scope inside of the controller, those properties are also accessed by the view.
In the view, you just refer to a property name, like {{state}} instead of using the prefix $scope,.
The scope has properties, which are shared with both the view and the controller.

Example (Scope Properties)

```
<!DOCTYPE html>
<html>
<script
```

```
src="http://ajax.googleapis.com/ajax/libs/angularjs/1.4.8/angular.min.js"
></script>
<body ng-app="exampleApp">
<h1>{{shape}}</h1>
<div ng-controller="exampleCtrl">
<h1>{{shape}}</h1>
</div>
<h1>{{shape}}</h1>
<script>
var app = angular.module('exampleApp', []);
app.run(function($rootScope) {
   $rootScope.shape = 'circle';
});
app.controller('exampleCtrl', function($scope) {
   $scope.shape = "square";
});
</script>
</body>
</html>
```

Output

circle
square
circle

Filters
Filters format data in the application. AngularJS includes several filters to transform data:
- orderBy Orders arrays.
- currency Formats numbers to currency.
- date Formats dates.
- filter Selects parts of an array.
- number Formats numbers to strings.
- json Formats object to JSON strings.
- limitTo Limits strings or arrays, to specific numbers.
- lowercase Formats strings to lower case.
- uppercase Formats strings to uppercase.

Adding Filters to Expressions

Filters can be added by placing a "pipe" symbol | in front of the filter. In this example, we will look at a filter for uppercase letters:

Example (Filters

```
<!DOCTYPE html>
<html>
<script
src="http://ajax.googleapis.com/ajax/libs/angularjs/1.4.8/angular.min.js"
></script>
<body>
<div ng-app="exampleApp" ng-controller="personCtrl">
<p>His  nickname is {{ last_name | uppercase }}</p>
</div>
<script>
angular.module('exampleApp', []).controller('personCtrl', function($scope) {
    $scope.firstName = "eBook",
    $scope.last_name = "Reader"
});
</script>
</body>
</html>
```

Output

His nickname is READER

Adding Filters to Directives

Filters can be added to directives, like ng-repeat, by using the pipe character |, followed by a filter:

Example (Adding Filters to Directives)

```
<!DOCTYPE html>
<html>
<script
src="http://ajax.googleapis.com/ajax/libs/angularjs/1.4.8/angular.min.js"
></script>
<body>
<div ng-controller="namesCtrl" ng-app="exampleApp" >
<p>Looping with objects:</p>
```

```
<ul>
  <li ng-repeat="x in names | orderBy:'state'">
    {{ x.name + ',' + x.state }}
  </li>
</ul>
</div>
<script>
angular.module('exampleApp', []).controller('namesCtrl', function($scope) {
    $scope.names = [
        {name:'Lisa',state:'Illinois'},
        {name:'Carl',state:'Marylad'},
        {name:'Susan',state:'Texas'},
        {name:'Lisa',state:'Georgia'},
        {name:'Mick',state:'Massachusettes'},
        {name:'Gary',state:'Florida'},
        {name:'Marcia',state:'Louisiana'},
    ];
});
</script>
</body>
</html>
```

Output

Looping with objects:
- Gary, Florida
- Lisa, Georgia
- Lisa, Illinois
- Marcia, Louisiana
- Carl, Marylad
- Mick, Massachusettes
- Susan, Texas

The "Filter" Filter
The "filter" filter is used to parse subsections of arrays.

Example (Filter Filter)

Filter names containing "e":

```html
<!DOCTYPE html>
<html>
<script
src="http://ajax.googleapis.com/ajax/libs/angularjs/1.4.8/angular.min.js"
></script>
<body>
<div ng-app="exampleApp" ng-controller="namesCtrl">
<ul>
  <li ng-repeat="x in names | filter : 'e'">
    {{ x }}
  </li>
</ul>
</div>
<script>
angular.module('exampleApp', []).controller('namesCtrl', function($scope) {
    $scope.names = [
        'Teri',
        'Carl',
        'John',
        'Gwyn',
        'Joe',
        'Marc',
        'Sarah',
    ];
});
</script>
</body>
</html>
```

Output
- Teri
- Joe

Custom Filters
By registering a function called a "filter factory" with your module, you can create your own custom filters: In this example, we will create a unique filter that will make every other letter uppercase.

Example (Custom Filter)

Create the custom filter, "exampleFilter":

A Code-Like-a-Pro Guide for AngularJS Beginners

```html
<!DOCTYPE html>
<html>
<script
src="http://ajax.googleapis.com/ajax/libs/angularjs/1.4.8/angular.min.js"
></script>
<body>
<ul ng-app="exampleApp" ng-controller="namesCtrl">
<li ng-repeat="y in names">
   {{y | exampleFilter}}
</li>
</ul>
<script>
var app = angular.module('exampleApp', []);
app.filter('exampleFilter', function() {
   return function(y) {
      var i, c, txt = "";
      for (i = 0; i < y.length; i++) {
         c = x[i];
         if (i % 2 == 0) {
            c = c.toUpperCase();
         }
         txt += c;
      }
      return txt;
   };
});
app.controller('namesCtrl', function($scope) {
   $scope.names = [
      'Jan',
      'Carl',
      'Maggy',
      'Heather',
      'Joe',
      'Gary',
      'Terrance',
      'Marc',
      ];
});
</script>
</html>
```

Output

- JaN
- CaRl
- MaGgY
- HeAtHeR
- JoE
- GaRy
- TeRrAnCe
- MaRc

Services

AngularJS uses individualized objects called services to perform specialized tasks. Filters and controllers rely on services on an as-needed basis. Services typically use the dependency injection mechanism. There are many services built in to AngularJS, such as, $route, $location, $window, $http, etc., each in control of a different task. The $http service, for example, contains everything necessary to access and collect data from a web server and pass it on to the $route service, which in turn defines it. You can also create custom services and reuse them throughout your code. Built-in services are easy to identify in code, because they always begin with the dollar sign ($).

Example (Service)

```
<!DOCTYPE html>
<html>
<script
src="http://ajax.googleapis.com/ajax/libs/angularjs/1.4.8/angular.min.js"
></script>
<body>
<div ng-controller="exampleCtrl" ng-app="exampleApp" >
<p>The url address of this page is:</p>
<h3>{{exampleUrl}}</h3>
</div>
<script>
var app = angular.module('exampleApp', []);
app.controller('exampleCtrl', function($scope, $location) {
    $scope.exampleUrl = $location.absUrl();
});
</script>
</body>
</html>
```

The url address of this page is:
https://angularjs.org/

The $http Service
The $http service is a commonly-used service in AngularJS. A request to the server is initiated by the service and the application handles the response.

Example ($http Service)

Request data from the server using the $http service:

```
<!DOCTYPE html>
<html>
<script
src="http://ajax.googleapis.com/ajax/libs/angularjs/1.4.8/angular.min.js"
></script>
<body>
<div ng-app="exampleApp" ng-controller="exampleCtrl">
<h1>{{exampleWelcome}}</h1>
</div>
<script>
var app = angular.module('exampleApp', []);
app.controller('exampleCtrl', function($scope, $http) {
  $http.get("welcome.htm").then(function (response) {
    $scope.exampleWelcome = response.data;
  });
});
</script>
</body>
</html>
```

Output

Welcome to AngularJS!

Asynchronous JavaScript and XML (AJAX) - $http

To get access to data in your web applications, the client must make requests to remote servers. With JavaScript, these are called AJAX requests. Using $http services, AngularJS makes AJAX requests for data from remote servers and returns a response to the application. AngularJS uses services architecture to support the AngularJS separation of concerns concept. It is good practice to make AngularJS AJAX calls by wrapping $http request into a factory and using it to serve data. This helps to keep your code more organized and separate the concerns. Also it allows you to pre-process the data and use it in multiple controllers.

Standard web pages interact with databases and servers by using an HTML form to execute scripts that GET and POST data to the server. The user clicks a button to send/get the data, waits for the server response, and views a new results page that has to be loaded in the browser. This process can be slow, especially when dealing with large files or great amounts of data.

By using AJAX, the JavaScript interacts directly with the server, using an XMLHttpRequest object. This allows a web page to make requests to, and get responses from web servers, without the page ever reloading. The user clicks a button that executes a script, and the results are shown in an HTML element that is identified by an ID.

```
<div id="ajaxResponse"></div>
```

Example (AJAX- $http)

Make an AJAX server request, and display the result in a header:

```
<!DOCTYPE html>
<html>
<script
src="http://ajax.googleapis.com/ajax/libs/angularjs/1.4.8/angular.min.js"
></script>
<body>

<div ng-controller="exampleCtrl  ng-app="exampleApp" ">
<p>The School message is:</p>
<h1>{{exampleSchools}}</h1>
</div>
<p>The School is closed today for rain.</p>
<script>

var sdntService = angular.module('schoolService', [])
```

A Code-Like-a-Pro Guide for AngularJS Beginners

```
schoolService.factory('schoolDataOp', ['$http', function ($http) {
 var urlBase = 'http://localhost:2307/Service1.svc';
   var schoolDataOp = {};
SchoolDataOp.getSchols = function () {
     return $http.get(urlBase+'/GetSchools');
   };
SchoolDataOp.addSchool = function (stud) {
     return $http.post(urlBase + '/AddSchool', schools);
   };
   return StudentDataOp;
}]);
```

Output

The School message is:

{{exampleSchools}}

The School is closed today for rain.

Methods
The example above uses the .get method of the $http service.
The .get method is a shortcut method of the $http service. There are several shortcut methods:

- .delete()
- .get()
- .head()
- .jsonp()
- .patch()
- .post()
- .put()

The methods above are all shortcuts of calling the $http service:

Example (Method)

```
<!DOCTYPE html>
<html>
<script
src="http://ajax.googleapis.com/ajax/libs/angularjs/1.4.8/angular.min.js"
></script>
```

```
<body>

<div ng-app="exampleApp" ng-controller="exampleCtrl">
<p>The School message is:</p>
<h1>{{exampleSchools}}</h1>
</div>
<p>The School is closed today for rain.</p>
<script>

var sdntService = angular.module('schoolService', [])
schoolService.factory('schoolDataOp', ['$http', function ($http) {
var urlBase = 'http://localhost:2307/Service1.svc';
   var schoolDataOp = {};
SchoolDataOp.getSchols = function () {
     return $http.get(urlBase+'/GetSchools');
   };
SchoolDataOp.addSchool = function (stud) {
     return $http.post(urlBase + '/AddSchool', schools);
   };
   return StudentDataOp;
}]);
```

Output

The School message is:

{{exampleSchools}}

The School is closed today for rain.

The example above shows the $http service using an object as an argument

Properties
The response from the server is an object with these properties:
* .config the object used to generate the request.
* .data a string, or an object, carrying the response from the server.
* .headers a function to use to get header information.
* .status a number defining the HTTP status.
* .statusText a string defining the HTTP status.

A Code-Like-a-Pro Guide for AngularJS Beginners

Example (Properties)

```
<!DOCTYPE html>
<html>
<script
src="http://ajax.googleapis.com/ajax/libs/angularjs/1.4.8/angular.min.js"
></script>
<body>
<div ng-app="exampleApp" ng-controller="exampleCtrl">
<p>Data : {{data}</p>
<p>Status : {{status}}</p>
<p>StatusText : {{ext}}</p>
</div>
<script>
var app = angular.module('exampleApp', []);
app.controller('exampleCtrl', function($scope, $http) {
  $http.get("welcome.htm")
  .then(function(response) {
    $scope.content = response.data;
    $scope.statuscode = response.status;
    $scope.statustext = response.statusText;
  });
});
</script>
</body>
</html>
```

Output

Data : Hello AngularJS Students
Status : 200
StatusText : OK

JSON

JSON (JavaScript Object Notation) is a format for packaging and storing data. An advantage of this format is that it can be understood by human readers.

As a simple example, information about me might be written in JSON as follows:

Example (JSON - Single Object)

```
var jason_Data = {
            "age" : "30,
            "city" : "Chicago, IL",
            "Name" : "John"
                    };
```

This variable has properties and values contained inside of the curly braces. These values can be accessed by calling the variable and specifying the property that we want to know.
A single variable such as this can include multiple entries by adding more curly braces, enclosing the object in brackets, and separating the objects with commas.

Example (JSON- Multiple Objects)

```
var jason_Data = [
{"Name" : "John"
 "age" : "30,
 "city" : "Chicago, IL",
},
{
   "name" : "Shelly",
   "age" : "20",
   "city" : "Atlanta"
}];
```

JSON can be expressed in complex, multiple arrays without compromising its simplicity and readability. JSON data can be stored on a remote and secure server, or it can be stored on a page in your web application.

Select
AngularJS includes dropdown lists based on contents in arrays, or an object. To create a dropdown list, based on an object or an array in AngularJS, use the ng-options directive to creating a Select Box by using ng-options.

Example (Select)

```
<html>
<script
src="http://ajax.googleapis.com/ajax/libs/angularjs/1.4.8/angular.min.js"
></script>
<body>
<div ng-app="exampleApp" ng-controller="exampleCtrl">
<select ng-model="selectedName" ng-options="x for x in names">
</select>
</div>
<script>
var app = angular.module('exampleApp', []);
app.controller('exampleCtrl', function($scope) {
    $scope.names = ["James", "Irving", "Shelly"];
});
</script>
</body>
</html>
```

Output

Events

Events directives signal the application to respond to changes in the environment. Some of the changes may be user initiated, others may be automated program functions. The following directives can be placed in your HTML to listen for events that your application can respond to.

- ng-blur
- ng-change
- ng-click
- ng-copy
- ng-cut
- ng-dblclick
- ng-focus
- ng-keydown
- ng-keypress
- ng-keyup
- ng-mousedown
- ng-mouseenter

- ng-mouseleave
- ng-mousemove
- ng-mouseover
- ng-mouseup
- ng-paste

The event directives enable you to call AngularJS functions at specific user events.

If you have both an AngularJS event and an HTML event, both events will take place.

Mouse Events

A Mouse event happens when the user' moves curser over an HTML element:

1. ng-mouseenter
2. ng-mousemove
3. ng-mouseleave
4. ng-mouseover
5. ng-mouseup

Or when the button is clicked on an element:

1. ng-mousedown
2. ng-click

Mouse events can be added to any element on the web page. We will examine the ng-click directive.

Example (Mouse Event)

```
<!DOCTYPE html>
<html>
<script
src="http://ajax.googleapis.com/ajax/libs/angularjs/1.4.8/angular.min.js"
></script>
<body>
<div ng-controller="exampleCtrl  ng-app="exampleApp" ">
<button ng-click="count = count + 1">Click Me!</button>
<p>{{ count }}</p>
</div>
<script>
var app = angular.module('exampleApp', []);
app.controller('exampleCtrl', function($scope) {
    $scope.count = 0;
});
```

```
</script>
</body>
</html>
```

Output

Although not rendered here, in your web browser, you will see a button. Upon clicking the button, the number below it will increase by 1incrementally.

Forms
The forms in AngularJS are used for validation of input controls and help with data-binding and. When a form object is found by the AngularJS compiler, the compiler uses the ngForm directive to create a form controller. The form controller object then searches for all input elements and creates the controls for each. What is required next is a data model attribute in order to establish two-way data binding, which will give the user instant feedback through the AngularJS validation methods.

Built-in Validation Methods
There are 14 built-in validation methods in AngularJS. These methods work well with HTML5 input elements and are dependable across all major web browsers.

Input Controls
The input controls are the HTML input elements:
- input elements
- select elements
- button elements
- textarea elements

Data-Binding
Input controls use the ng-model directive for data-binding.

Example (Form)

```
<!DOCTYPE html>
<html lang="en">
<script
src="http://ajax.googleapis.com/ajax/libs/angularjs/1.4.8/angular.min.js"
```

```
></script>
<body>
<div ng-app="exampleApp" ng-controller="formCtrl">
 <form novalidate>
  First_Name:<br>
   <input type="text" ng-model="user.firstName"><br>
   Last_Name:<br>
   <input type="text" ng-model="user.last_name">
   <br><br>
   <button ng-click="reset()">RESET</button>
 </form>
 <p>form = {{user}}</p>
 <p>master = {{master}}</p>
</div>
<script>
var app = angular.module('exampleApp', []);
app.controller('formCtrl', function($scope) {
   $scope.master = {firstName:"eBook", last_name:"Reader"};
   $scope.reset = function() {
      $scope.user = angular.copy($scope.master);
   };
   $scope.reset();
});
</script>
</body>
</html>
```

Output

First Name:

> eBook

Last_Name:

> Reader

RESET
form = {"firstName":"eBook","last_name":"Reader"}
master = {"firstName":"eBook","last_name":"Reader"}

Explanation
"Novalidate" disables default browser validation. The directive, **ng-app**,

44

A Code-Like-a-Pro Guide for AngularJS Beginners

defines the application. The directive, **ng-controller**, defines the AngularJS application controller. The directive, **ng-model**, syncs input elements the model. The controller, **formCtrl**, efines the**reset**() method and gives values to the **master** object. The method, **reset**(), makes the **user** and **master** objects equal. The directive, **ng-click**, calls the **reset**() method, if the button is clicked.

Global API

The Global API is a collection of global JavaScript functions that perform tasks, such as:

- Comparing objects
- Iterating objects
- Converting data

The Global API is accessed by using the angular object.

Common API functions:

API	Description
angular.lowercase()	Converts a string to lowercase
angular.uppercase()	Converts a string to uppercase
angular.isString()	If the reference is a string, returns true
angular.isNumber()	If the reference is a number, returns true
angular.lowercase()	

Example (API – Lowercase)

```
<!DOCTYPE html>
<html>
<script
src="http://ajax.googleapis.com/ajax/libs/angularjs/1.4.8/angular.min.js"
></script>
<body>
<div ng-app="exampleApp" ng-controller="exampleCtrl">
<p>{{ x1 }}</p>
<p>{{ x2 }}</p>
</div>
<script>
var app = angular.module('exampleApp', []);
app.controller('exampleCtrl', function($scope) {
    $scope.x1 = "MIKE";
    $scope.x2 = angular.lowercase($scope.x1);
});
```

```
</script>
</body>
</html>
```

Output

MIKE
mike

Includes
With AngularJS Includes, external HTML can be included on your web page. This is done by using the ng-include directive:

Example (Includes)

```
<!DOCTYPE html>
<html>
<script
src="http://ajax.googleapis.com/ajax/libs/angularjs/1.4.8/angular.min.js"
></script>
<body ng-app="">
<div ng-include="'exampleFile.htm'"></div>
</body>
</html>
```

Output

Include This Header

Routing
The ngRoute module allows you navigate to different parts of your application without the page having to reload. You can use the ngRoute module to route your application to various pages this way. To prepare your applications for routing, you must include the Route module:
```
<script
src="http://ajax.googleapis.com/ajax/libs/angularjs/1.4.8/angular-route.js"></script>
```
You must then include the ngRoute as a dependency in the application module:
```
var app = angular.module("exampleApp", ["ngRoute"]);
```

A Code-Like-a-Pro Guide for AngularJS Beginners

This enables your application to access the route module, using "$routeProvider" to map various routes throughout your application:

Example (Route)

```
app.config(function($routeProvider) {
 $routeProvider
 .when("/", {
  templateUrl : "main.htm"
 })
 .when("/1", {
  templateUrl : "file1.htm"
 })
 .when("/2", {
  templateUrl : "file2.htm"
 })
 .when("/3", {
  templateUrl : "file3.htm"
 });
});
```

AngularJS applications require a container (ng-view directive) to hold the data that he routing provides. Here we examine the ways to include this container:

Example (Container)

1. <div ng-view></div>

2.

3. <div class="ng-view"></div>

AngularJS only allows one ng-view directive per application. This is the placeholder for all of the views provided by the route.

$routeProvider

Using the $routeProvider, you can delineate what page to display when a certain link is clicked.

Example (Route Provider)

```
var app = angular.module("exampleApp", ["ngRoute"]);
app.config(function($routeProvider) {
  $routeProvider
  .when("/", {
    templateUrl : "main.htm"
  })
  .when("/1", {
    templateUrl : "file1.htm"
  })
  .when("/2", {
    templateUrl : "file2.htm"
  });
});
```

The $routeProvider is defined by using the AngularJS config method. Processes loaded into the config method are performed as the application loads.

Controllers
Using "$routeProvider" you can also assign a controller for each view for the client.

Example (Add Controllers)

```
var app = angular.module("exampleApp", ["ngRoute"]);
app.config(function($routeProvider) {
  $routeProvider
  .when("/", {
    templateUrl : "main.htm"
  })
  .when("/1", {
    templateUrl : "file1.htm",
    controller : "londonCtrl"
  })
  .when("/2", {
    templateUrl : "file2.htm",
```

```
        controller : "file2Ctrl"
    });
});
app.controller("file1Ctrl", function ($scope) {
    $scope.msg = "This is file1";
});
app.controller("file2Ctrl", function ($scope) {
    $scope.msg = "This is file2";
});
```

The "file1.htm" and "file2.htm" are standard HTML files, to which you can add expressions the same as you would with any other HTML sections of your application.

Templates
You can use the template property to code HTML directly into a property value..

Example (Template)

Write templates:

```
var app = angular.module("exampleApp", ["ngRoute"]);
app.config(function($routeProvider) {
    $routeProvider
    .when("/", {
        template : "<h1>Main</h1><p>Click on the links to change this content</p>"
    })
    .when("/apple", {
        template : "<h1>Apple</h1><p>Apples are red.</p>"
    })
    .when("/orange", {
        template : "<h1>Orange</h1><p>Oranges are orange.</p>"
    });
});
```

CHAPTER 7: PUTTING IT ALL TOGETHER

We will now build a complete AngularJS Application. We are going to create a simple list of students wherein we can add or remove individuals:

My Student List
- Michael
- Trina
- Jill

Add students here
Add

Getting Started:
Start by making an application called studentList, and add a controller named exampleCtrl to it.

The controller adds an array named students to the current $scope.

In the HTML, we use the ng-repeat directive to display a list using the students in the array.

Example (Student List)

At this point, we have made an HTML list based on the students in an array:

```
<script>
var app = angular.module("exampleStudentList", []);
app.controller("exampleCtrl", function($scope) {
   $scope.students = ["Michael", "Trina", "Jill"];
});
</script>

<div ng-app="exampleStudentList" ng-controller="exampleCtrl">
   <ul>
     <li ng-repeat="x in students">{{x}}</li>
   </ul>
</div>
```

Adding Students:

Add a text field to the HTML, and link it to your application by using the ng-model directive.

Make a function in the controller, and name it addStudent. Use addMe as the value of the input field, and add an item to the students array.

Add a button that includes the ng-click directive. This will run the addStudent function when the user clicks the button.

Example (Add Students)

Now we will add items to our student list:

```
<script>
var app = angular.module("exampleStudentList", []);
app.controller("exampleCtrl", function($scope) {
   $scope.students = ["Michael", "Trina", "Jill"];
   $scope.addStudent = function () {
      $scope.students.push($scope.addMe);
   }
});
</script>

<div ng-app="exampleStudentList" ng-controller="exampleCtrl">
   <ul>
      <li ng-repeat="x in students">{{x}}</li>
   </ul>
   <input ng-model="addMe">
   <button ng-click="addStudent()">Add</button>
</div>
```

Removing Students:
We need to be able to remove students from our Student list.

Make a function in the controller, named "removeStudent." This will accept the index of the student you want to remove as a parameter.

Make a <span> element for each student in the HTML, and give them an ng-click directive that initiates the removeStudent function with the current $index.

Example (Remove Students)

We can now remove students from our Student list:

```
<script>
var app = angular.module("exampleStudentList", []);
app.controller("exampleCtrl", function($scope) {
    $scope.students = ["Michael", "Trina", "Jill"];
    $scope.addStudent = function () {
        $scope.students.push($scope.addMe);
    }
    $scope.removeStudent = function (x) {
        $scope.students.splice(x, 1);
    }
});
</script>

<div ng-app="exampleStudentList" ng-controller="exampleCtrl">
    <ul>
        <li ng-repeat="x in students">
            {{x}}
            <span ng-click="removeStudent($index)">&times;</span>
        </li>
    </ul>
    <input ng-model="addMe">
    <button ng-click="addStudent()">Add</button>
</div>
```

Error Handling:
The application has some errors, like if you try to add the same student twice, the application crashes. Also, it should not be allowed to add empty items.

We will fix that by checking the value before adding new students.

In the HTML, we will add a container for error messages, and write an error message when someone tries to add an existing student.

Example (Error Handling)

Our student list can now write error messages:

```html
<script>
var app = angular.module("exampleStudentList", []);
app.controller("exampleCtrl", function($scope) {
    $scope.students = ["Michael", "Trina", "Jill"];
    $scope.addStudent = function () {
        $scope.errortext = "";
        if (!$scope.addMe) {return;}
        if ($scope.students.indexOf($scope.addMe) == -1) {
            $scope.students.push($scope.addMe);
        } else {
            $scope.errortext = "The student is already in your Student list.";
        }
    }
    $scope.removeStudent = function (x) {
        $scope.errortext = "";
        $scope.students.splice(x, 1);
    }
});
</script>

<div ng-app="exampleStudentList" ng-controller="exampleCtrl">
    <ul>
        <li ng-repeat="x in students">
            {{x}}
            <span ng-click="removeStudent($index)">&times;</span>
        </li>
    </ul>
    <input ng-model="addMe">
    <button ng-click="addStudent()">Add</button>
    <p>{{errortext}}</p>
</div>
```

Design:
Our application is now functional, however it needs a better design. If you do not want to spend a lot of time designing CSS, go to http://www.extractcss.com/, and select styles that will be automatically converted into CSS format for you.

Tips for Implementing AngularJS

AngularJS is regarded as a scripting language that simplifies coding and expands the range of possibilities for web-based user interactions. Despite its many, useful built-in features, AngularJS is not a perfect fit for all web application development. Games and GUI editors, for example, require applications with advanced manipulations of DOM elements. These kinds of apps are Generally, CRUD (Create, Retrieve, Update, and Delete) database apps are the best fit for AngularJS. In these cases it may be better to use an online library with a lower level of abstraction, such as JQuery.

- Separate app logic scripts from DOM manipulation scripts. This can help to make your coding structure more suitable for testing.

- It is helpful to separate the client side from server side during app development. This allows you to reuse both sides of your code for other, unrelated development projects.

- Use frameworks for UI design, logic modeling, and app testing to guide you through the process of app development. This will save you a lot of time and energy; no need to reinvent the wheel.

- Use bootstrapping to auto-inject premade online services and features into your app. This helps you to implement features more quickly. This will also spare you from having to write pages of initialization code in an effort to get basic features working.

CONCLUSION

Thank you again for downloading this book!
I hope this book was able to help you to code like a pro!
The next step is to get to work on your first AngularJS web application.

Finally, if you enjoyed this book, then I'd like to ask you for a favor, would you be kind enough to leave a review for this book on Amazon? It'd be greatly appreciated!
Click here to leave a review for this book on Amazon!
Thank you and good luck!

www.ingramcontent.com/pod-product-compliance
Lightning Source LLC
Chambersburg PA
CBHW061040050326
40689CB00012B/2909

* 9 7 8 1 5 3 7 4 6 4 6 8 8 *